EARTHLY GODS

Earthly Gods

Copyright © 2024 by Jessica Nirvana Ram

LCCN: 2024937977
ISBN: 978-1-955602-18-1 (paperback)

Published in the United States of America

Published by Variant Literature Inc
Graham, NC 27302
www.variantlit.com

Cover Design by Hafsa Khan
hafandhaf.com

Table of Contents

Table of Contents Continued

Advanced Praise

Jessica Nirvana Ram's *Earthly Gods* wrestles the angel of belief to our mundane sphere, incarnating as devotion to divinity and ancestors, shifting into a love wincing from the searing beauty of the world. From the tender renderings of a grandmother's praying hands to incantations to the departed to the rivers that are the women throughout this book, these poems teem with diasporic wonderments and heartaches. Rituals described and deities invoked, Ram's debut chants the sincerest ode of my own heart as the speaker prophesizes, "The marrow of your bones will sprout dandelions." All I can see after reading this is a summer field filled with small petaled suns lifting up their heads from the green in praise.

—Rajiv Mohabir, author of *Whale Aria*

In this remarkable debut, Ram maps a new kind of coming of age and reckons—through exacting narrative and inventive approaches to form—with the renovations required in divining one's own mythology. As these poems tend gender, culture, and inheritances of many kinds, they also lend rare and well-crafted insight into how language accompanies us into a future we couldn't know to expect.

—Meg Day, author of *Last Psalm at Sea Level*

In *Earthly Gods*, Jessica Nirvana Ram writes about family and legacy, religion and friendship, grief and food and sex and love, always love, with joy and wisdom and generosity and humor. She wields sensation—color, flavor, sound—like a painter, and she wields emotion just as deftly, moving in a few lines from gratitude to loss, from longing to sorrow, from pain to praise. The world is somehow made more vivid and arresting in these gorgeous, gripping poems, and as we read them, we are nodding and crying, we are laughing and snapping, newly aware of the richness and complexity of our own lives. This is a lush and layered debut, meant to be savored, in service of anyone who ever tried to figure out how to honor their inheritance and go their own way.

—Melissa Crowe, author of *Lo*

Emotionally complex but clear-eyed, Jessica Nirvana Ram's poems hurtle through 'acres of ache' in search of 'a balance, a boundary.' Familial love amends and troubles. Grief is non-linear. Tradition enriches and separates. The language—gorgeous, incisive—braids shadows, lights. Bewilderment is transformative. Joy ripples with possibilities. Ram possesses an emotional and linguistic intelligence that startles the senses, that invigorates the heart.

—Eduardo C. Corral, author of *Guillotine*

I.

"we exist between
a self for self and a self for others"

—Aja Monet

88-01 88th Street

after Aja Monet

grandma's hands were an oiled comb
through my black hair, a twist of the wrist
to curl the ends. they were the pointa broom's
coconut branches dusting hardwood,
& baby powder on my brother's behind.
her hands were a belna pressing dough
into rounds, clapped roti over the kitchen sink,
spoons of dhal over white rice. shaky handwriting,
a slow looped R, mouthing uncertain hindi
alongside bollywood subtitles. her hands were
palms pressed together, hummed mantras, agarbati
circling mourtis. grandma's hands kneaded skin
& carried sleeping bodies. they were spare dollars
for churros & italian ice, rite aid gum & a bucket
of KFC. her hands were my hands as I taught myself
to pray again, in the quiet of my apartment.

Unripe Child

In Queens, my grandfather's garden stretched
around our little corner house. I used to climb
over the brick stairs' railing by the front door
to hover over his plants. Life rose into the world
over & over before my eyes.

Sometimes I'd gather tomatoes & peppers
into a large silver bowl, eyeing the green,
unripe tomatoes, desperate to pick them,
slice them open, see if they were green inside, too.

From the ripe tomatoes my grandmother would
make paste to use in stewed chicken or saltfish.
I would sit & watch, little fingers stretching
& asking constantly if something was ready,
if I could help.

But in the kitchen we couldn't rush things.
Curries needed to simmer, to reduce & thicken.
& for roti, you have to let the dough rest once
after mixing flour, water, baking powder, & salt,
& again after separating into sections.

When I am in kindergarten my teachers tell my mother
they want me to skip first grade. She does not tell me
about this until I am in college, says: *I wanted you to be
the age you were then, because you would never be it again.*

Did her insistence on taking time push me to impatience?
It's not like she was wrong. Mothers, of course, are almost
never wrong. But I was restless, never learning how to hold
onto things, how to let them grow. Even now, I kill
nearly all the plants I touch.

Once, in third grade, I went to school with my thick curls
brushed out, a bush on my head, & the boys laughed.
This is where I begin to sour, learn quickly how to tame
the excess of myself, my hair in a ponytail or straightened
through high school.

I became familiar with the smell of singe, with the hour it took
to break my hair down. An unwanted kind of patience.
Who exactly was I slowing down for? I think this must have
confused my mother. To see her child whose eyes once glinted
& widened when she spoke, folded in on herself—
an unripe tomato retreating to rot instead of bursting into red.

Her ripe child lives tangled in the back of my throat.
Wrapped with foliage & withered stems. Sometimes
I cough up dried flower petals, pick thorns from between
my teeth. Sometimes, I hear the child humming, softly.
& I want to hold her, let her out of this barren body,
but I think we're both scared of who we'd become
if we were set free.

Miracle Fruit

The first time I thought I was pregnant I ate a whole
pineapple. Swallowed handfuls of sesame seeds, let a papaya
rot on my writing desk, quietly counted my wire hangers.

I was terrified & broke & even after all three tests
ran negative, our room still smelled like pineapple,
& I prayed for blood.

We learned to laugh about it, our childishness,
how our tongues bubbled from too much fruit,
how I should have at least toasted the sesame seeds.

Over our six years together, we'll have more scares,
but I will not tell him. I will hold my stomach at night
knowing there is a chance someone like me is growing.

Notes on Being Purple

I am echoed royalty, saturated satin,
a nebulous blotch of body decorated
with bruises, a watercolor wasteland
of lilacs & violets; I am

picked morning glories, love
as a lullaby or a cursed tongue
dipped in plum, staining
the insides of my mouth.

I embody it all, like the middle
of the flag I hide, my second childhood
bedroom, walls washed in eggplant
& lavender or the dress

my grandmother bought
from the flea market, how I grew
until it split, until they had to peel it
off my widening frame.

I am purged red-purple wine,
the blue-purple sky after death;
the sound of incense, of poetry.
I am too many parts withered,

hung & drooping like wisteria,
a walking omen. If I slip out of skin
& undress before undrawn blinds,
watch girl bloom into jellyfish.

Body ninety-eight percent water,
two percent nerves. Fold me into
a wreath, into a weapon. Purple poison,
the shade beneath my eyelids

when I pass out & dream in mauve.
If I give myself permission to love
in purple, I fear I'll bleed out. Blue-purple
red-purple purple-purple.

Instead, beneath the pyre, my body becomes
burial ground, a place to leave offerings,
where purple prayers press into purple-girl flesh,
& my skin turns amethyst, crystalline, permanent.

While Making Laddoo for my Cousin's Wedding

It takes my mom & me hours
to roll the darkened flour
& crushed cashews
into recognizable mounds,
cardamom dusting our fingers
& the countertop,
sugar tinging our tongues.
She asks midway through the process
if I'd want to live with someone before
marriage & I say yes.
She is displeased with this,
believing there is joy in discovering
a partner in a new shared space
but I say, I don't want to be surprised
after I've committed myself.
She asks what happens if things end
before a wedding & I say,
we will deal with it if it comes.
Her lips tighten, eyes fixed
on shaping the laddoo between
her palms, the sphere holding
under the pressure of her hands
& if there's not enough
mixture it is too dense
& when there's too much
it comes apart & we can tell
which laddoo were our firsts
& which ones came last
& there are nearly a hundred
sweets stacked in the aluminum tin
& I remind my mother
how costly my wedding will be
because I am her only
daughter & I have known
my whole life that this wedding

would be as much hers
as it would be mine & I am praying
to only do it once, in all its glory.
From the evening of the dig dutty,
her wrapping earth in a shawl
planting the foundation of my new
life, to the hours being mehendied
all along my arms & legs,
every room packed with our family,
anyone she wants & everyone
I need & Ma—
don't you think I want this love
to be sure so we can do this
the way you've dreamt it?
We reach the end of the ladoo
mixture & I consider asking
if she could love another
daughter the way she would
a son, but I refrain,
ask if she thinks we've made
enough & she tilts her head
counting, says
it is enough, for now.

Reciprocity

When I'm undressing my grandmother
for bed, we take breaks so she can
catch her breath & I see how small
she is. Her arms droop, hang like loose
dough, her stomach stretches to kiss
the brown, rippling skin of her thighs.
Some nights she doesn't look at me
when I kneel to peel her socks off.
Instead, folds her hands together
in her lap, lets her head bend toward
the ground as if in prayer, & whispers—
Me used to do this fuh ayodeze.

I say, I know, while unscrewing the Vicks'
by her bedside, camphor & menthol
settling over me as I rub her chest & back,
massage it into her shoulders. She breathes
slowly, the water in her lungs bubbling
into the air like a toy whistle. Some days,
when she is more ocean than woman, her ankles
swell like pufferfish & I knead my knuckles
into the soles of her feet, hum the lullaby
she used to sing to put me to sleep:
        chandaa mama door ke.

Tucked between the pages of her bhajan book,
there's a picture of me & my grandfather, his legs
outstretched on the bed, my toddler arms
reaching for him, palms pressed to the skin
of his calf, his smile wide & warm. Months ago
when I took my grandmother to the hospital
after signs of a stroke, I tucked her book alongside
a change of clothes. Carried them from hospital
to hospital until they confirmed the bleeding in her
brain. After a nap one day, when we knew the bleed

had reduced in size, she told me my grandfather
visited her dreams & she turned him away. She laughed,
Me nah ready fuh go nowhere.

While she remains upright I take her blood sugar,
prick whichever finger she offers, squeeze
the wrinkled skin until the red stains the white
test strip. I lost my fear of needles after
my grandfather's third stroke, after I ran
out of dollar bills for rehab center vending
machines & found myself confined to sterile
rooms where I could do nothing but study
the bodies of the people who raised me
& wonder who I looked most like. My
grandfather's skin was dark from years
of heavy sun on sugarcane fields, his hair tight
& coiled. Grandma's skin was fair, her hair
straight & black. I had his curls & her cheeks.

Before my grandfather's last relapse, he made
my mother promise him that she'd take care
of my grandmother & she, of course, said yes.
Some days I take her yes, cradle it in my arms
& sing it a lullaby. I want to tell her, *this yes*
belongs to me too, Ma. The week before
my grandfather died I went to see him,
took his hand, made him the same promise.
I swallow it whole, keep it between us.

Before she lets me lay her back into bed,
my grandmother tells me again about
the mango trees, the cows that came
when she whistled no matter how far they'd
strayed, her belief that she'd done everything
for her seven children, even if they didn't
always call her enough. I listen, no matter
how many times she repeats,
                    I've had a good life.

She slows with time & I ask if she's ready
to sleep. She nods & I tuck her body into
the bed, kiss her forehead, & turn the lights
out when I leave the room. I can hear her
reciting her prayers behind the closed
door. When I make it upstairs my mom
is waiting for me & I tell her grandma
is taken care of. I can see the breath
she's holding leave her body & I ask
if she wants me to bring her tea to her
bedroom. She says yes, & leaves me
in the kitchen while the water boils.

Contract for Assimilation

after Hans Christian Anderson

Ma, were you scared? Did you wait
until you were certain you'd be having
a daughter before you approached her?

I imagine the sea witch loomed, her eyes
half lidded, lips curled as she hummed
at your request. Another voice for her vault,
another immigrant mother seeking a gift,
only to leave with a well dressed curse.

Ma, I am foreign in every space I inhabit.
When our family makes music with their creole
I wilt, keep myself folded & shut, listening
with fervor but aware, always, to never open
my mouth. It doesn't come out right. I am
a skipping record, a tape unwound & tangled,
unrepairable.

When the little mermaid signed away
her tongue & tail for something glittering
across the waves her terms were no secret.
She accepted every step feeling like a thousand
knives, that she could never return to her old life,
that she very well might fail.

I can't break a contract I didn't sign. Can't return
to myself what was taken. How do I measure
the worth of sacrifice? Am I allowed to both
be grateful & to grieve? I have not yet
turned to seafoam but some days my tongue
is a bed of needles & I am hollowed
& I am trying not to blame you.

i am unfit to raise daughters

i've always wanted children / at first / sons / sons are less likely / to inherit my mouth / stuffed full of cotton balls / slicked with gasoline / tongue clipped & hung / on a clothesline / waiting for a matchstick / a hose / a body to slip back into / i thought / i could clad sons in an armor / built of my bones / tie their wrists with / yagnopaveetham woven from veins / sew the gayatri mantra / onto the roof of their mouths

maybe / i believed / i could raise / honeysuckle sons / with sugarcane limbs / their sweat would taste / like rose water & jasmine / their blood / condensed milk & clove / with sons / i hoped / i could rest easy / because / with daughters / i will come undone

split at the spine / daughters will inherit the fire / i've always swallowed / kept tamed / in the pit of my belly / they will / like kali maa / emerge from my forehead as / my wrath / bathed in blood / striped red & brown / crimson glistening under moonlight / tiger skin / a mark of their mother

i know / sculpting shields is a waste of time / so i will carve spears / from clavicle / crown them with a wreath / of cervical vertebrae / my daughters will wear / a garland of my lungs / strung together / with braided strands of dark hair / i cannot raise them to be / like me / to be like a mother / whose hands shake / like hummingbird wings / a blur of body / undeserving of holding / life / like theirs

let me offer them / instead / chambers of my heart / sliced into thirds / laid atop red hibiscus & lentils / if they press into tender muscle / their fingers will stain with / me / i suppose / i fear daughters / because / i am / an unsteady stack of organs / masquerading as / lethal weapon / unrelenting fury / when really

i am nothing but / paper & ink / flammable & temporary / a vessel to bring them into / this world / who / upon giving birth / may very well / shudder & shatter / into ash

Self-Portrait as Depressive Spiral

Malicious spirits, I can handle, wayward
souls I escort easy. But you haunt me
in ways I cannot exorcise. Living at
the back of my throat reeking of rot,
metastasizing at night. I can feel you
crawling down my esophagus. I heave
over the side of the bed & you hang
onto pink muscle like lifeline.

You want to string my body into
a malfunctioning marionette. I want
to tell you that you do not own me.
I light agarbati, weave smoke into
window crevices & door hinges, repeat
the gayatri mantra like an unravelling
ball of yarn, as if prayer could reach
through my skin & lure you out.

You settle into the gaps of my spine,
bloom beneath each rib until I am bloated
& bursting. If I stop fighting, you'll force
fractures until I spill from every fissure.
So I carve incantations into the soft flesh
of my forearms, drown in rose water,
beg for something holy to save me. Still,
you echo within me, promising to stay.

Patchwork

Embroider the word *burden* to the underside of your tongue.
Let it tug your flesh, a swollen raincloud, a threat.

If you ask for help you admit weakness, tear the wound
open. Don't part your lips, hide your marred mouth, gums

all battered & blue. If you open for them, you might die.
This may seem drastic but it's always been life or death.

You are woven to sink spools of thread in stomach acid.
To bury stitching patterns in the marrow of your bones.

There's risk in revealing. That's what you've been told.
It doesn't matter if you bleed out, if you fracture.

Some days it will leave you brimming with excess,
others barren & aching. Stick your tongue out in front

of the mirror. Follow the lines, swing from *b*'s curves
to *n*'s arch, try to remember what it felt like without it.

Can you remember? You must have been a child, still
mouth wide & yearning. Unpricked. A stranger to blood.

You know there is no returning, no before waiting
on the edge of an undoing. But some days you want to

tug at the string. Threaten to undo the word, free yourself.
Sometimes you hook it to a tooth & pull, wondering how

you'll unravel.

Untethering

Locked in a death march toward the river's edge,
my body spills, splits against the water's surface.

I fear sinking. I wonder if he knows how heavy he is,
how certainly we'd drown if he couldn't let go.

I want to apologize for expanding beyond us, ballooning
from his lungs & reaching for the atmosphere.

Does he know how long I've been worried about the day
I would undo our seams & soak into the earth?

The day he'd no longer be able to run his fingers
down my spine & ask for forgiveness.

To love him is to be bound. To be moored to a version of me
I no longer recognize. I don't know how to tell him

I am oversaturated with myself.
I have no more room for him.

Jellyfish Girl

Last night I woke up part jellyfish,
tentacles wide & transparent,
head bulbous like a moon jelly.

I told you not to touch me. Swam
away from our bed until I was sea deep
in myself, floating among the blooms
of jellyfish watching them brush up
against each other, no harm no screams,
just soft touch, comfortable sparks.

I wondered if I'd ruined myself
by becoming this way, if your eyes
would always be rimmed with fear
& trepidation, with some need to trap me
in a bathtub or a tank, to keep me
at arms length—

you've never been good at swimming
& you don't like the ocean. We both know,
I cannot live in your cupped palms.

Notes on Searching

When I am young, I run
hands over my rounded belly,
coat it in a layer of soap
as I shower, faucet off & dripping
against the tub floor, echoes
of cars & bicycle tires & heavy laughter
spilling in through the bathroom window.
I take a finger & carve an outline
of an Om into the sudsy canvas
of my stomach.

I don't think I knew god yet,
but this was what holy looked like,
something I could memorize,
form with my own hands.

Om is the sound
of the universe, I'm told.
I wonder if it is the only sound
the universe makes, if ever
the hum of mantra echoes
like a sob, goes silent like
a strangled breath, screams
& howls like thunder,
like a splitting tree trunk, like
the earth opening to swallow us.

I spent years denying god
but even then, I listened
closely to rivers, the Schuylkill
when I am young & infatuated,
the Susquehanna, when I am young
& in love, the Cape Fear
when I am grown & out of love

& every time the water itself
reached toward me, a constant.

I etched Om after Om into the margins
of my notebooks, inked the insides
of my wrist with ball-point, perhapsed
that if I listened long enough, kept my lips
pressed together, it would make itself known.

I did not believe in god but god
kept coming, in the wind
as it whistled through drooping
branches, in the persistent rain
that begged me to soak in it,
in the electric sky when it split
across the horizon.

I know now that god believed
in me. Believed in my windswept
& chaotic hurricane of a self,
my measurable threat. Believed
that in the eye of my storm I'd find
calm, in the middle of the winds
I'd hear it. I'd hear it.

88-01 88th Street, pt. 2

after Aja Monet

Grandpa's hands were sugarcane fields
& bottles of rum,
mounted shoulders & loose change
for ice cream after school
or chocolate coins
from the drugstore,
they were paint cans
& slabs of wood, gardening tools
soaked in earth, the pungent smell
of alcohol noosed around
you know me love you,
they were chest deep rumbling laughter,
mumbled-beneath-the-breath jokes,
they were all these things before
the oxygen tanks, cycled-through
rehab centers, vacant stares—
I remember the Woodhaven fair
that one cold February,
just the two of us,
when I made him try deep fried Oreos,
sugar dusting his jacket after the first bite,
how he chuckled softly,
how he smiled at me.

notes on orange

grandma's dimpled smile & how it reminds me of soft caramels / hands pressed to my cheeks / thai chicken curry / red paste & coconut milk / simmering to feed friends on my apartment floor / ginger tea for strained throats / henna stain before it darkens red / all soft tangerine on brown skin / grapefruit rind / peeled mangoes / the sweetest ones messy & soft / juice spilling down your chin / chicken alfredo & too much paprika / pumpkin cooked down with dhal pouri / my aunties' bara / their polouri / pennsylvanian autumns / route 15 in october driving home from college / the week my grandfather died / how the leaves had just begun to change / sweet potatoes under roasted marshmallows / candy corn & carved gourds & Reese's wrappers / diwali / diyas beneath my grandmother's altar / how I used dollar store candles when I celebrate alone / phagwah like the festivals I dreamt of / my face only knew talcum powdered gestures / jalebi / sticky spirals / sugared mithai / like the ones I packed / in little gold boxes / for my cousin's wedding

Wedding Night

My cousins were surprised to see me sleeping
on the couch beside the bride the night before
the wedding.

They assumed I'd be like my mother or rather,
who they believed my mother to be, that I'd need
space on a bed somewhere, a room to myself
in this house full of two dozen bodies. But the bride
needed me & I was more familiar with floors
than they'd ever know.

My aunt asked me quietly in the half lit hallway
if I would stay with her daughter & who am I
to say no?

The bride laid on a foam insert pushed up against
the wall, her skin slick with turmeric & ghee
so in the morning she'd glow the way a bride
was meant to glow & the responsibility was mine,
to rub her skin again, spreading the yellow paste
along her brown forearms & thighs, soft circles
against her cheeks & forehead—

I wondered who would caress my skin like this
when I got married, if there would be anyone,
if it would fall to my mother.

In the morning I massage her body once more
before she showers, paint her nails, dress her
like a doll between my hands until she is beautiful
& red & everything her mother dreamed of.

II.

"i am part machine / part starfish / part citrus / part girl / part poltergeist /
i rage & all you see / is broken glass"

—Franny Choi

On Good Tongues

My grandmother tells me *you need a good tongue*
in life, you gotta show love with it, you gotta demand
love with it. In the same breath she reminds me
of the benefits of drinking Ovaltine before bed,
how remembering to heat my milk first is key
& I tell her

        yes, I know. Like a promise,
like a prayer. I do not tell her how often
I hold my tongue, I do not tell her I cannot find Ovaltine
in my local markets. I only tell her yes—

                is that not what it means
to show love with this tongue, to lie for her sake? Her joy
is so dependent on my insistence that I am in the kitchen
every evening dressed in garlic & onion & oil. That I wake
in the mornings to incense smoke & god

                on my tongue &
I do not tell her about the heartbreak until it is over. I tell her
about cut flowers I buy myself from the grocery store,
how they'll sit on my table for weeks, mimicking life
even though they've long died, brittle bones on the brink
of collapse, until I remember to take them out with the trash
& then I do it again.

        I cannot keep plants alive, it is a testimony
to all I did not inherit from my grandmother, her hands so eternally
wed to earth. Her South American soil birthed vegetables, nurtured
a livelihood. I believe her body is bound in Guyana in a way
it could never be bound in the States. I wonder often
if a part of her

        is already buried there & when her legs give out
from a fall I think, yes, it must be. Yes, fragments of her
are scattered about & calling on me. Some days I breathe
her in more than others & when I pray it's her voice,
not mine

that echoes in my apartment.
When I leave my partner of six years, I apologize
for choosing myself over us, but if I am to demand love
with this tongue, I cannot swallow myself
whole for anyone else.

                    When I visit home,
my grandmother asks me about marriage,
about children, & I tell her *not yet. Remember*
what you told me about getting my education?
How no one can take what's inside of my head?
& she says

                              yes, I remember.
But her hands tremble & I know she wants to give me
a wedding before she dies & I know, she will not be able
to give me a wedding before she dies so yes,

                              I lie to her.
I lie about Ovaltine & the plants I've killed & the love
I left because

                    I am too much
like her. A woman so bound by what she believes
she must do that no one but the gardens she's tended
hear her cry & I want to ask my god how much
of that land is salted with her tears but I refrain
because god will not tell me & my grandmother
will not tell me & I cannot show her these hands
I am trying to build a life with, how they are so much
like dried up riverbeds, like barren soil because we
are nothing if not withholders

                    of loss.

Fragmentation

I once got my head stuck
in playground bars, at the park
two & a half blocks from our house,
the pressure a red throb, building
as I screamed.

My grandmother stared up at me,
her voice straining to reach where her
hands could not. Someone called
the fire department but she'd soothed me
before then, talked me through wriggling free.

As we walked home I rubbed my ears,
they felt warm & pink & I wondered
what I'd look like had I lost them.
Would my hair have been thick enough
to hide my lack of lobes?

Maybe they'd have sewn them back on,
or gifted me the loose clumps of flesh,
as a memento.

When I am in Sixth Grade a Boy Calls Me Octopus Hair

The boy is small & faces me with sharpened teeth.
I could never name the look in his eyes but I could always

smell the bloodlust & that day, he spewed incantation
against the sea monster living on my head & my body

awoke, tentacles sprouting from skin darting out in defense
of this small girl's self. I watched as newfound limbs

reached out to suffocate him, pressing into the small boy's flesh
until it puckered red with suction cup rings, until he screamed

& hissed & threatened me with those shark teeth of his, thrashing
about in my grip. I bared my own beak, burst through his paper

flesh, saw my fury reflected in his fear soaked irises as he realized
he was not the predator here. Maybe I should have warned him,

should have let him know that my kind happily devours his kind,
that even though I specialize in camouflage, or could easily offer up

a spare limb & make my escape, I am fucking tired of disappearing
when provoked, tired of folding into this small body, tired of sacrificing

pieces of myself as if to say all of me
isn't worth fighting for.

Self-Portrait as Manic Episode

I nose dive off moon craters into pockets of black holes,
siphon stars & collect them in tear ducts & the bends
of elbows. I am hollowed & holy, a mess of molecules
& light skirting the corners of my lips to the underside
of my fingernails. Watch me pluck Saturn's rings, wear
them as bangles. They'll clink & chime against one another
echoing between ribs. Last night I strung Jupiter's moons
into a pearl necklace & swallowed it whole. Listen to the
way they pinball around my body, settling between shoulder
sockets & spinal shifts. Tomorrow, I'll weave earrings
from the Northern Lights. How I've always loved their milky
emeralds, watercolor wisps like loose ribbon pulled
across the horizon. Everything vibrates when I'm like this,
humming lips pressed to my neck, & the floor splits open,
showing me god or a field of marigolds or my mother's arms
& I let myself fall, descending like Icarus all caught up
in the way my feathers glimmer with wax & sunlight—
I am warm & awake & reaching, an apocalypse brimming
on my wingtips.

my heart is a slippery fish

fillet it / cut the cheeks out / & see / they'll be tender / keep the blade close / to bone / clavicle to tail fin / pull clean through flesh / separate into slabs / to be swallowed / seasoned / skewered / skin crisped in skillet / body flaky & boneless / marinate the head & skeleton / for bouillabaisse / a thick stock / pick your teeth clean / with pin bones / see how many pieces / this heart is capable of / becoming / dissected devotee / I promise / there is no waste here / if you catch me / you can use it all / every last scrap

The first time I said I love you—

I lied.
This is not admission that I never
loved you. I loved you. But the first
time it slipped casually off your tongue
your cheeks went stuttered salmon,
pupils into pufferfish, fingers already
laced into mine tightening like netting
& my chest bloomed into morning
glories, a field of them, purple & pink
& soft & I knew you meant it.

The first time I said it back it was
an echo, a ricocheted frequency
because the longer I didn't say it
the wider your whirlpool gaze
grew. I was afraid I'd be swallowed
whole, drown in your wanting
& maybe you would have waited,
my fear unfounded, but as long as
we're being honest here—I lied twice.
The first time I said I love you
& also the last.

I bracketed us this way because
both times your heart weighed
more than mine on the scale we
shared. If I didn't add an arm,
some extra ribs, a smattering
of teeth—we'd never have evened
out. It took leaving to realize
I was a dismembered delusion,
a halfway ghost body sacrificing
for scraps.

to the conquerors

your eyes are drenched in hunger,
a desperate lust. you have an appetite
for my lesser-ness, my otherness,
as if indulging in this brown body
could satisfy you.

bite my flesh & off comes
my grandmother, calloused feet &
peppered tongue. you'll spit me out,
say I burn your throat, say you need
delicate & docile. I'll never go down easy.

sink teeth into my palms & find
my grandfather, all sharp knuckled
& stoic, smelling of powder & earth
& liquor. you go for my stomach, meet
my grandmother's mother, small statured
& big bellied, her womb once home
to seventeen begging mouths.

tilt my neck & blood spills down your
gullet until you choke on indentured
servitude, your eyes rolling backwards
toward the boats my ancestors rode
across the oceans.

you'll never be full, tearing away at my skin
& muscle until you're sucking on the marrow
of my bones, hearing my aunties chant obeah
on you & your kin.

the body of me will haunt you, live in
your ribcage & dance on the underside
of your eyelids. I'll ring in your ears,
I'll follow you to death & every breath after.

On Inherited Rage

When my brothers scream
their hoarse voices ricochet
up the staircase, heavy boots
on hardwood, bodies barreling
through the house like full scale
earthquakes. They embody
their anger, wear it on their necks
like a trophy.

I never raised my voice,
carried my anger in my fists
out the door, threw the basketball
in our driveway, over & over
until I'd calmed down.
I remember the way the ball hit
the pavement, slicing through
the silence of the suburbs.

Sometimes I'd lay on the driveway,
especially in winter, swallowing
the cold until I could barely think,
tracing the shape my breath took
in the air above me.

I can't remember the last time
I held a basketball, if I attribute it
to anger now, to some sense of loss.
The other day, I sat on the floor
of my apartment, bones bubbling,
a stark humming in my chest
& I kept hearing rubber on asphalt
on a loop, until I could pinpoint
the feeling as anger, could say aloud
this is anger, I am angry.
Was I allowed to be angry?

I look up boxing classes,
imagine what it would be like
to be out of breath, to hear
my heart thrumming in my head,
to push away this feeling
I was never taught to deal with.

I don't like anger I don't know
anger. I am uncomfortable with
anger & all its weighted risks.
When I'm angry I cry, I burst
like a shaken soda can.

It's easier to walk away,
to break open parts of my body,
waterboard my brain with distractions,
basketball or boxing, something physical
& all consuming.

I remember the day my brother's ex
cheated on him. How he brought
his fist to mirror, shattered
the whole thing
& I wonder what all I've broken
that can't be collected into a dustpan
or replaced.

I wonder who's coped better
after all these years, but then
he calls me crying & screaming
his voice burrowing into me
& I think this is something
we've both failed at after all.

touch starved

phantom hands   hold my face steady & i close my eyes
like someone's there,   like i'd let this ghost body
take me if it wanted to. i fall   into nothingness,
cannot tell   if i am dreaming anymore
because my body begs   to be touched—
along the crook of my neck,   length of my spine,
the soft of my stomach, & between   my thighs—
& before i know it   i am acres of ache,
my own hands   never enough.

tonight my limbs pulse   i wonder if there's something
squirming inside me, if releasing it could   stop this spiral
of senses & i sit   on the kitchen floor, head in my palms,
when my veins start humming, body becoming
an orchestra.   i take a wire scrub from beneath the sink
& rub & rub & rub   until my forearms are raw,
& i cry   because i am turning the only body i have
into patchwork.

in the morning i survey the damage,   treat the wounds,
paint the abrasions   to match my skin. i cannot let anyone
know i've been whittling myself down, how would i
explain myself?   i remember the feeling of unfurling
beneath someone else's touch   but i have never been soft
with myself & i feel   unable to start learning now. i wonder
what this means. if my ragged hands   will be the reason
i cannot survive   myself.

river woman

where does the river run?
                              I point to my sternum
& you pry open my ribcage, release a stream
of salmon, silver spilling steadily towards sky

one leaps into your palms & you split it
along the spine, its pink flesh beckoning you,
soft & bright; set its halves on my waiting thighs,
skin to skin

you reach between my breasts, become
soaked & slippery swallowing mouthfuls
of woman, drowning in this catastrophe

I imagine you want to know how to stop it,
the spillage—love, I am nothing but excess
& I tried to warn you before the undoing, I did

you promised you could swim, said you were unafraid,
I believed you & unfurled

You've Gone Pink

I put flamingo feathers bouquetted at your doorstep,
wrapped watermelon flesh around your taffy tongue,
left you sticky & soaked licking fuchsia up my forearm.

Breathe in our euphoria but keep those bottled magenta
mornings away from me, shoved into the back pocket
of those jeans you've torn but won't toss. I want you

to let go, but you sink into this, into us. You tattoo me onto
the split flesh beneath your winter burned cheeks, stain
your skin a busted bubblegum. You turn pink, soaked in cheap

champagne or that bottle of rosé you tried to refuse. You look
at me & I remember your blushed breathing, nails burrowed
into my shoulder, how in that moment I still loved you.

& now, you've gone pink. Like up-all-night irises, like my first
stuffed animal, neck wrung with ribbon. I watch you,
eyelashes blossoming into carnations, pastel petals

over hooded eyes. Come candy mouthed, all puckered
& popped. Come into me, again & again. This time I'll be
the one to swallow you whole & you can watch how sunrise

pools into seawater, how I cup it between my palms, drink
its salt, its rose quartz beading across my knuckles. Unhinge
your jaw for me, play pretend, believe you are forgiven.

Soulmate

In Greek mythology, Zeus severs humans
into two parts. Together we'd be too powerful.
Instead, we spend our lives searching—& yes,
I saw myself as half of a whole. Pushed my body
into others' to see if we'd fit, offered my heart
as a consolation prize.

When I finally find a boy with ice cap eyes,
we combine. Amalgamate into a brimming beast
of loose limbs & looser definitions of love. We
barreled through years together, mowed down
anyone who questioned the way his mouth
morphed over mine or how my hands braided
themselves behind my back. My mobility
was irrelevant. I would have let him encase me
in his body if that's what he wanted. I couldn't
imagine a life with one heartbeat, one pair
of palms pressed together. I didn't want
to go back to the before, that's what I kept
telling myself
                    & then,
spaces began to grow between us, slowly
at first. Like stretching gum. Pulled fibers
fringing at the edges. I began to feel lighter,
floating almost. I wiggled free a leg, an arm,
disentangled my hair, our fingertips. He did
not notice until there was nothing but a thread
left & there I was, with scissors. Wondering
if I could fly without him. If I wanted to.

I cut. Watch as he sinks without me. Feel feathers
blooming between my shoulder blades. I measure
the clouds, the taste of ascension faintly familiar.
& some days, yes, I miss it. The weight of another
body, but never enough to dive back down.

Incantation to the Departed

When I drive past the body of a deer
sometimes whole, sometimes not, flesh
matted with tire tracks, hide & fur
melting into the asphalt, eyes glazed
& star searching—I hear them.
Which is to say, they are welcome here.

They enter through the toes, take comfort
in the lining of my stomach, the caged warmth
of my chest. They often vibrate amongst
my vocal cords. I will hold them for as long
as they need. How could I purge a soul
that doesn't belong to me?

My faith urges me to offer a prayer,
to repeat mantras over the deceased,
to find their loved ones & offer company.
Because there must be someone waiting
for them to come home, & grieving is softer
with those who know loss.

In high school, a classmate of mine was hit
by a car. Ever since, a wooden cross dressed
in flowers & ribbons perches at the top of a hill
on the side of the road where his life was taken.
I didn't know him, but after all the afternoons
I've driven past, I've gotten familiar with the energy
of his memory & I wonder, what our highways
would look like if we planted a flower in every
location that's known death. A tribute to everything
lost, with something birthed.

When someone in my family dies, we mourn
for days. We gather on the floors of each other's
homes, sit crosslegged, singing as though they
can hear us—because we know, they can hear us.
We are loud & grieving & have no shame.

So forgive me for thinking death deserves more.
Forgive me, those who've passed through this body
if ever I've held you for too long.

The Day We Watched My Grandfather Burn

Pews line the crematorium, the space too small
for all the funneling brown bodies. We spill into
the aisles, linger on stone steps.

Moving towards the coffin I clutch clipped carnations,
petals coming loose in my palms & I remember
Kuch Kuch Hota Hai, the opening scene one of death.
Body in casket, encased in wood like a second veil,
a slow burn in the middle of a stretch of land. But here,
at the Fresh Pond Crematorium in Middle Village, NY
we are entrapped by walls & ceilings. We are confined.

As flowers get dropped around the body my mother
tells me this is kindling, a way for the fire to catch.
Pandit circles my grandfather's corpse with tinder,
the cadence of his prayers echoing around me. I can
feel my grandmother's sobs in my own chest. I do not
know how to comfort her.

After prayers, the coffin is wheeled down a hallway
& some of us follow. Others watch through a newly
revealed glass wall. We leave grandma with the others,
her heart too at risk of bursting if she were to get this close.

Honestly, I didn't know what to expect. My grandfather's skin
had begun to gray, his eyes sinking into his skull. I know that
means we must do this soon. At the end of the hallway
there's a polished, golden bar separating us from a wall
of square openings, the man who had led us here a level above.

My grandfather's mahogany coffin slides into an open square,
a bouquet of funeral flowers balanced atop the curve of closed
casket, & a glass fixture that reminds me of a moving chalkboard
is wheeled in front of the opening.

You may press the button when you are ready.

Collectively, we all look at each other. Realize, suddenly,
that his final moment will come by our hands. One of us
needs to push the red button resting in the middle
of the golden bar. There is a flurry of uncertainty.
We are all inexperienced in death here.

Then, without warning, I watch my uncle's finger descend
on the trigger. The coffin is abruptly, violently engulfed
in flames. The orange & yellow blooming against the glass
that keeps the fire from our faces, but not the heat, the finality.

My mother collapses in my arms & I find myself shielding
her eyes as she screams, *take me with you. Please take me
with you.* I hold her & watch the people I love crumble
around me. I only wish I'd had arms to hold them all.

How to Discard Offerings

After my first puja, the first one I could call
my own at twenty-two, I surveyed the aftermath.
Carnations threaded into garlands,
their loose petals a flurry of reds & whites
beside cotton balls stained
with ghee & turmeric & vermillion.
Everything from the altar, the mix of kindling
from the fire, the ashes, the laddoo & parsad—

I remember the pujas of my childhood,
the tied grocery bags of offerings
hooked into the grip of an aunt as she left
our New York home or
the water kissing my grandmother's ankles
as she let a wrapped cloth of puja offerings
drift out into the Schuylkill river just down
the road from our Pennsylvania home.
I remember sometimes
the way red would leak from the bags
or the cloth, how its trail would linger
& linger until we were out of sight.

I held my own offerings between my fingers,
jasmine & camphor punctuating the air.
My mother told me I won't be a bad Hindu
if I chose not to let these things loose
into the Schuylkill.
I laughed because I am still trying to learn
what it means to be spiritual,
how to do all this correctly.

Our ancestors used to let their offerings
spill into their rivers because
their groups were small, would only feed
the water food & flowers & soil it could swallow
heartily, could accept as its own offering—
the whole act one of gratitude
for sustaining life.

Now, temples in India have begun to dig pits
deep into the earth for all the aftermath,
so it gathers & grows & recycles
itself into manure, into something life giving
because the Ganges
has had enough.

When I pray now, in the quiet
of my apartment, when I make offerings
on the holidays I have gotten used to spending
alone, I think about the Cape Fear river,
how it pulses with chemicals & I cannot drink it
& I slip my measly offerings, soft petals & incense ash,
into a pot of soil. Consider if this honors earth,
if in turn it must too honor water.
I want to believe the definition of holy
can be of my own design.

Afterimage

The people I love most in this life are yellow,
butterscotch & honey laughter, lemon sour
comebacks, goldenrod & turmeric hearts.

They don't always start yellow & not everyone stays
yellow & you surprised me, the dial on you turned
like you'd been storing pigment in your balled up fists

& your yellow was sudden & all encompassing,
like looking into the sun & you stayed that way
even after you killed yourself.

The daffodils you left in my apartment were yellow, too.
Beautiful & arranged in old wine & glass coke bottles,
my dollar store vases. Six bouquets. You'd thrown yourself

a funeral in my bedroom & I'd thanked you for it. A consolation
prize for loving you or an apology for leaving. But the night
they told us you were dead I wandered for hours before

coming home & my door jammed. It didn't want to let me in
& when it finally opened there you were, waiting for me.
A smear of yellow. A sobbing echo.

Heart Rot

Sometimes trees die from the inside out,
when fungi whispers through wounds
in the bark, aiming decay at the heart.
From the outside you can't tell until
one day, amidst its weakest moment,
the tree topples into waiting earth,
the sound of crackling branches
its last words.

Mothers too, harbor heart rot. Swallow
back blood, stand tall to feign strength.
My mother misunderstood, believed
presenting herself as flawless was what
I needed as a child. I cannot blame her.
See, her mother carried forests in her
footsteps even when her feet bled &
her body heaved from all the birth & loss.
Her lush fingertips sprouted carnation
blossoms, tongue dripped with sweet sap.

When my mother is only a daughter,
she sees the splinters left littered
around the house. Notes the piles of rot
mixed in with all the mulch. Maybe this
made her believe it was better to choke
back the death. Maybe she didn't want
to see it, & in turn didn't want to show it.

How could she have known I had
begun to decompose, perishing
in the corner of my room? Considering
all the ways in which I could make
the decay speed up until I toppled
into earth.

I wonder, now, about the state
of my own heart rot, about the ways
in which I too, have learned to cut
back death. I dream of a future
where I can saw off a small section
of my core to gift to my children to say:
look my loves, look at all my death,
look at everything I fight against &
see how I still find ways to live.

We Were

We left cabbages in checkout lines,
noticed missing vegetation too late,
set the whole week off kilter. We were
future planners, we were hopeful. We
pulled the Four of Wands on a New Moon
& cried on our apartment floor. This was
a good sign, a centering, an affirmation
of sorts. We called our mother by cup phone,
strung the line from North Carolina to
Pennsylvania, unrolled our connection
between major highways & car pileups.
We offered her gold & garnish, she took
specks of iron from our blood instead,
searching for origins, a past-life callback
from when we were once stars. At night we
sautéed ourselves in honey & soy sauce,
decorated tongues with red-pepper flakes
& undressed apologies. She never believed
us & we were never surprised. But it was
easier to lie, then. To blame forgetfulness,
to blame the swiftness of a day, the fleeting
space of language. It was easy. We believed
it was easy. We offered up our skeleton as
a xylophone & were left with echoes of body,
a cacophonous aftermath to living like our
skin & organs belonged to someone else.
We were still givers, then. We tied our soul
to a kite that day & wished for the best. We
think it was for the best.

Crimson Girl

I want red to be ruby & roses & royalty, chiltepin peppers & my aunties,
all their full bellied laughter, wrinkled hands & darkened bindis.

I want my wedding saree, my sindoored scalp. Oh, I've dreamt of it,
scarlet woven with gold, crimson girl swathed in promises—

but then I say girl & become stoplight, cherry cheeks smeared
& sunken, sharpened acrylics severing burgundy skin. I burrow

into myself again, tearing out veins like loose wiring. I am not
a girl here.

                                        I am a massacre.

My red is swallowed violence, cranberry vodka vomit, the lights
in the bar bathroom, how they turned my palms into crime scenes.

I am splitting my heart, gouging it open like my grandfather's tomatoes,
pressing thumbs into its middle, raw muscle turned pomegranate.

The space between my breasts becomes furnace, untamed flames
like untrained hands & my throat goes blood moon, tongue red velvet—

why is it, I am always the one coming undone?

III.

"I am a threat.
And full of grief even.
In my joy."

—Kaveh Akbar

When the Air is Heavy

I.

Count to three. Repeat the gayatri mantra over
& over while you will your body to rise. Light
agarbati, circle your mourtis, yourself,
every corner of the room. Carry the smoke
counterclockwise until the whole apartment
smells of incense. Gather it up, send it out
the front door.

II.

Open the blinds, turn your palms towards light,
let morning glories sprout from your fingernails.
If you escorted the right bodies out the door, hum
something grounding like Solange's Cranes in the Sky
or You Are Enough by Sleeping at Last, coat the air
in begging breaths until the only thing soaked into
your walls is you.

III.

Ask for love. Really, I mean it. Bleed into your phone
& watch how it blossoms, brims with a softness
you are new to—but be honest, it is starting to feel
familiar. Being loved. Isn't it strange? It took losing
the person you used to call love for you to really find
it. All that time you were cradling fool's gold. Look,
you've always deserved more.

IV.

Try something new. Clear quartz. Tarot cards.
Talking to a younger you. If you go really far back
you might find a small girl with supernovas for eyes
& she will scare you. Let her. Take her hand, follow.
She'll show you everything you've ever buried &
she'll ask you to forgive yourself.

V.

Forgive yourself.

VI.

Dress yourself in onion & garlic & oil until
your apartment smells like home. Add spice.
Tongue the heat & exhale. Soothe with sugar,
condensed milk & bread (like your mother) or
hazelnut chocolates. Punctuate the evening
with black tea, brown sugar, & cream.

VII.

Talk to god. Or the moon. Both are good listeners.
Track the cadence of your voice & pay attention
to the echoes. Does it still sound like you? Dab
rose water on the four corners of your bed. Sweep
the kitchen, vacuum the living room, read poetry
as if it were gospel. (It is.)

VIII.

Know, my love, that this is temporary. The heaviness,
& the clarity. In each cycle make tallies of all the ways
you've learned to love yourself. May you never run
out of tallies.

After Crying at 3AM I Wake Up to a Poetry Reading & Remember

This is my church. Poems
my offerings, decorated
with garlands, anointed
with rose water
& jasmine oil. If I circle
them with incense,
the smoke skips
like a metered line, like
enjambment, like music
& muscle memory.

I can be my own
altar here. I can be
holy, too.

Divine Contrapuntal

I am learning how to be soft
how to swallow the edges, to exhale
a part of me I'm unfamiliar with
these hands are ragged from care
& the ways I've been wrung dry
I am terrified to be honest with you
sacrifice is woven into my spine
if I could call upon all my stray selves
like Durga I'd manifest
a goddess unstoppable & full

even on days when I renounce it
my body roots itself, digs in, reaches for
something tangible, a fixed feeling.
forgive me if I'm tired of it, of others
I'm trying to find a balance, a boundary but
it is too much to ask of myself, I only know
excess is buried between my ribs
let me request of Shiva his trident
& show what combined power can do
I am slayer of demons, divine

astral ashes

twenty-four hours / of fire / reduce / bones, teeth, & hair / to a refined powder / while blood, skin, & organs / all dissipate / slowly / into the atmosphere / my grandfather's ashes / live above my grandmother's fireplace / for three days / before his ghost / inhabits her dreams / before he carries them to / nightmares / he pleads / *let me go, take me to water* / the distant coasts of Guyana / beckoned his soul / after three years / in a functionless body / three years sewn / into a hospital bed / he ached / for the warmth of home / for sugarcane soil / creole tongues / he was impatient / & I do not blame him / my grandmother tells me / about the importance of returning / the body to water / how letting the remains / of death / be washed away in ocean / allows the soul / to travel anywhere in an / instant / it makes me wonder / where he must have went / first / whose dreams he slipped into / how he must have / stretched his legs / in relief

earthly gods

one /

my belief in god comes from / my grandmother / but let me be honest / for so long / i could not believe in god / instead put my faith / in her devotion / her unwavering / hands clasped / in the way mantras lived on her tongue / she told me / *when you have* / *no answers* / *close your eyes* / *& pray* / & please / forgive me for saying she / was my first religion

these days i keep my god / pressed between my collarbones / traced into the palm of my hands / i hold them beneath my tongue / they are with me / swaying in the empty of my apartment / to the symphony of late nights / heavy sobs / my god & i / we whisper to each other / when i cannot sleep / & i am grateful

two /

i could not always / sense the dead / but my father / grandson of a priest / speaks with them / tells me when i was an infant / his father's ghost / stood by my crib until my little face / scrunched red with fear / how he said *okay* / *you've seen her* / *now go* / how my mother was easily afflicted by spirits / but could not see them / & for a while / they came to bother me as well / smothered me in nightmares / until my father circled my room / my body / with incense / until he guided them away from me

i live alone now / no one escorts my ghosts / out the front door / so i learn how to know they're there / i cannot see them / but they surround me / weight in the air / taffy in my throat / ears that won't pop / i write them away / turn poems into prayers / prayers into poems

three /

i hum when i cook / & this / comes from my mother / but okay / here's the thing / so much of me comes / from my mother / i do not know if i can catalogue it all / if i should even try / but i will try / because i am stubborn / & that too / comes from her she tells me of guyana / how she once wrote a poem / won a contest / was asked to read it when they unveiled the new bus station / in her village / & she was too scared / to do it / she often wishes she'd held onto that poem / when she is pregnant with me / she writes a letter to an unborn daughter / after twenty-seven years i still don't have the letter / but she has given me the ability / to write things into existence / & she told me once / *parents* / *are our earthly gods* / i watch as she bathes her mother / bowed at her feet / & suddenly / i imagine my mother / myself bowed at her feet

My psychiatrist tells me breakups are the closest thing we have to death

& I think about the last funeral I went to, the eulogy I wrote,
the bodies I cremated & suddenly you're there & I'm wrapping
you in kindling, decorating your body with anniversary letters
& old photographs (your sister's wedding, the gallery openings,
graduation). I toss in the stuffed animal you wanted to return
the day I left, there are books & clothes & promises & they all
burn quick.

I never wanted to light you up, to hold your ashes in my palms
but the fire swallows the pieces of us, catches in your hair. I smell
singe, track the flicker of flame across your irises & I do not
recognize you.

This was the body of a boy who was no longer obligated to love me.
Your hands didn't reach for my face but instead, barreled towards
my gut to pull at my organs—like the sight of me coming apart
fulfilled you.

I am no stranger to fragmentation, my love. I know what it means
to carve myself up as an offering. I'm not saying it was right
or enough, but it was how I loved you. & now, there are pieces
of me buried beneath your ribcage, stuffed between the spaces
in your spine, & if you need to—keep them.

I have a proposal. I'll write a eulogy for the version of you that loved
me. I'll mourn him because he was the one who drew hearts on pizza
boxes every Valentine's Day, who added Bollywood music to his
study playlists, who carried all of my firsts in his fists. That boy
surfaced at the end of it all, envisioning our wedding (one ceremony,
not two right?) all the while I was scouting escape routes.

I'll scatter the ashes in a river, set him free. I'll show you
what it means to be without me.

From Under the Cork Tree

We are not children anymore, we are, by every right,
adults but—
                    note the childlike joy of a windows-down car,
early days Fall Out Boy turned all the way up, heads
bobbing en-route for milkshakes & cajun fries & yes,
we sat & ate until our eyes glazed over with the need
to be horizontal, & I melted into couch cushions
upon returning to the soft quiet of my apartment,
giggling as memories of lobster lifespans & outer space
jellyfish & ceiling fan mechanics flooded me & yes,
none of it matters so all of it matters & believe me
when I say I am high on joy, heavy with it & I may not
have your kind of church with pews & prayers but this,
this feels pretty close, this hymnal of laughter so blooming
& full-bodied my head throbs—
                                        I find god in these moments,
& listen, I'll be honest with you, I never thought I'd live
this long, never thought I deserved friends that loved me
like this, that choose me over & over again & forgive me,
I'm trying to learn how to honor that, the care,
how to say listen, I promise, I am grateful, know I am
grateful & god, if you're listening, if you're there—
let me have more of this, let me be worthy of this.

On Accepting Blessings

I am standing in front of my new Corolla,
pink lengha skirting the pavement,
wearing slippers that don't belong to me
as my pandit unwraps cubes of camphor.
He begins, eyes forward, voice soft:
> *Place fragments of camphor around the vehicle,*
> *by the tires,*
> *in front of & behind the car.*
> *Set the limes directly in the path of the tires*
> *so when you drive forward they'll be crushed.*

We are in daylight, on the street outside
of my aunt's home in Yonkers, all our brown
so unabashed—
& I am ashamed of my shame.
Of the way my eyes catch drivers & sidewalks,
of my fear that they see me & feel disgust,
that I fit their image of me, that my otherness
scorches their skin.
I want to conjure a cloud around us
but there is no room here.

My aunt is spiritual, heavy in heart & faith,
eager for my willingness to accept blessings,
so she asks for this & I oblige. Once, when the darkness
took form & tied itself to my limbs, she came bearing
rose water & a golden Ganesh pendant strung
onto a beaded red chain.
He became my tether, hanging from the rearview
of my car, traveling in my pocket through airports—
so I could clutch the beads during takeoff.
My grandmother tells me he is known
for both removing & placing obstacles
yet, I try not to ask for anything. All I do
is tell him about my day
& call this prayer.

Pandit dips his fingers into turmeric,
touches the door handles, draws a swastika
on the steering wheel, the bright yellow crossing
over the silver Toyota logo. He leaves a lime
dipped in the powder in my glove compartment,
& tells me:
>   *Remove it after twenty-one days.*
>   *Clean the whole car after twenty-one days.*
I don't tell Pandit I brush the swastika away
later that week when I take my car for service.
I can't admit aloud to him that something holy of ours
will always be mistaken for hate.

We move to the front of the car & pandit continues:
>   *Break the coconut now,*
>   *pound it into the pavement*
>   *so we can douse the car with its water.*
It takes me three hits before the shell fractures
right down the middle,
you can hear the eyebrows raise as it does—
my aunt's laughter heavy in the air,
that's my girl.

For the longest while I called myself culturally religious
because I believed more in my grandmother
than god. It was easy to see holy in the commonplace,
in the ways agarbati smoke sifts skyward
& turns my ceiling into a morning fog, how lemon
slices placed for protection around a room rot
& need to be replaced, a small mortality. How the comforters
we lay across living room floors during puja smell sweetly
of softener & fire.

After Pandit sprinkles coconut water over the car
& asks me to prop the hood, he instructs:

64

> *Balance the halves of the fruit on the car's*
> *front bumper,*
> *Drop camphor pieces inside the white flesh*
> *& light it, ignite all the scattered fragments*
> *one by one.*

As if to create a barrier around this Corolla of mine,
as if to say, *darkness, you've no place here.*
I'm watching the fire burn,
the yellow swastika pandit traces onto my engine
looks prosperous, looks holy
in the way it should as it sits upright, not tilted
on an axis. It is the middle of the day
in the Bronx, I've got on socks with sandals
& the brightest pink Indian wear,
coconut water splashed along the fabric,
& I am feeling eyes that don't exist.
I am feeling otherworldly & vulnerable.

I am wondering if questioning is allowed here.
I know it is—
but I don't ask.
I get into my car, fix my gaze on
Pandit & my aunt as they tell me:

> *Drive forward.*
> *squish the limes,*
> *take a lap around the block,*
> *keep the windows down.*

The camphor is fragrant on my fingers
as I navigate these unfamiliar streets.
My family knows I'll be leaving home soon,
the want of safety so imbued with love,
& I come to a realization—
I never really stopped believing.
I thought I did, in the days when my body & bed
became one. In the days when tomorrow
only lived as a maybe. But even in all that haze,
I believe my grandmother when she jharays
my body for evil eye, whispering quickened

prayers & teaching me ones to recite
when I walk through dark places alone.
I believe my father when he says I'm like my mother—
easily agitated in the presence
of spirits, when he tells me about the palpability
of the dead, how the hair on his forearms stand
when there's someone heavy in the air,
when he carries them away & leaves
a room lighter. I believe in lemon slices
over entrance ways, in rose water
on the four corners of the bed,
in the quicksilver I keep in my purse.
I believe.
      I believe.
           I believe.

When the tires roll back into the driveway,
I watch my Ganesh swaying from the rearview,
his gold catching in the light.

Duplex

I was wrong about how I wanted to be loved.
I thought what we had would always be enough.

     If I hadn't changed, would it have been enough?
     The woman in the mirror hasn't touched you.

The man in your mirror hasn't touched me.
Maybe we are loving each other's ghosts.

     What does it mean, to love each other's ghosts?
     Should I, after all this time, have been mourning?

After all this time, I have been mourning us.
This shouldn't surprise me, I know loss well.

     This loss shouldn't surprise me, I know you well.
     This is enough for you, it always has been.

For you, I am enough, I always was but
I was wrong about how I wanted to be loved.

Ars Poetica

Poem dresses well,
shows up at my front door
with carnations & chocolates.
Poem promises me a lovely evening
& I am entranced by their sugared
tongue & low whisper.

Poem has skin like cardamum & clove,
says my name like they've known it
their whole life. Poem puts a hand
on my back, lips to my ear,
says   *open,*
& I do.

Poem ribbons around me,
snakelike but still measured.
Poem has hasty palms, like they want
to own me. I let poem own me.
Poem says   *good,*
                                  be good.

& I am, for a while. I give poem the reigns
to my body & they twist me, twirl me,
turn me into their puppet.

But poem forgets I am stubborn
& I keep trying to look poem in the eyes,
to read their hollowed irises, swallow
their hushed lips. Poem does not
like this. Grip tightening around my jaw,
mouth to ear again, harsher this time
but still low & vibrating through me,
poem says   *no,*
                                  eyes forward,
                                  be good.

& I bite poem on the shoulder. Poem laughs
into the crook of my neck, breath all smoke
& embers, hands loosening around my waist.
Poem still does not let me look at them,
but they keep holding me, humming
into my skin & I say   *thank you.*

Ode to Self

Have the audacity to love yourself & your body will split,
shed heartbreak like loose hair on your bathroom floor.

The marrow of your bones will sprout dandelions—be strong enough
not to call them weeds because even weeds, my love, are bright & soft

& living & who needs function when there's beauty? It'll be uncomfortable,
not like snakes in your throat or tumbleweed in your stomach but

more like fuzziness on your tongue when you can't remember someone's name
but they're familiar. Reacquaint yourself with the curves of your cheekbones,

how they remind you of your grandmother. Study the darkness of your eyes,
like tree bark, like soaked soil. Your eyes reflect you & you them

& here you stand in an endless loop of selves & you are not desperate
for anyone else. It is bizarre, to reach your hand toward the mirror,

fingertip to fingertip, & whisper

I know you,

I know you.

in lieu of a poem—

sautéed cabbage over corned lamb,
how it reminds me of my mother
& marries well over rice;
spinach shrunken & soaked with garlic,
the way my grandmother likes it;
brussel sprouts bursting with balsamic;
broccoli heads splitting like lumber
beneath my knife, brushed with olive oil,
soaked in heavy cream;
green onions clipped with scissors
over tom yum; roasted asparagus resting
beside fillets of salmon;
julienned green peppers for fajitas,
the recipe from my ex, the only one
he knew & I kept;
the smell of rosemary & patchouli,
how it reminds me of love,
not his, just love, familiar warmth;
french gardens; lemon verbena leaves
in water; bouquet garni in the coq au vin;
fresh pesto ground in pestle & mortar,
all heavy pressure & pocketed laughter;
never jealousy, no, not that,
only girlhood & the feeling of stretching;
a crown of vines or the mountainsides
in Provence or Pennsylvania,
New York or North Carolina;
think roots; think Guyana's flag;
grandfather's green thumb
& pistachio pocked palms;
the five dollar bill framed
above the doorway in our first home,
a gift from my uncle to my mother,
a wish of wealth & prosperity,
how it hung there until we moved;
my parents' worn wedding tape,
their stilled smiles; something holy.

Notes

The section one epigraph is from Aja Monet's poem "footnote" in her collection *My Mother was a Freedom Fighter*.

"88-01 88th Street" and "88-01 88th Street, pt. 2" are after Aja Monet's "564 park avenue"

Agarbati is the Guyanese-Creole word for incense used in prayer.

Roti is an Indian flatbread.

Laddoo is an Indian dessert.

In "Reciprocity" the line *"chanda mama door ke"* comes from a Hindi lullaby, roughly translated to "oh, my darling child."

"Contract for Assimilation" uses inspiration from Hans Christian Anderson's original "The Little Mermaid."

In "i am unfit to raise daughters" there is reference to Kali Maa who is a Hindu goddess. She originally appears as emerging from the goddess Durga as the manifestation of her rage. She is known as the goddess of death and rebirth.

In "notes on orange" there's reference to a route 15 which is located in Central Pennsylvania.

Diwali is a Hindu holiday, the festival of lights. Diyas are the small candles lit during Diwali.

The section two epigraph is from Franny Choi's "Turing Test" in her collection *Soft Science*.

"When I am in Sixth Grade a Boy Calls me Octopus Hair" plays on the fact that octopuses have been found to eat sharks both in aquariums and in the wild. I first found out this fact through watching an episode of Naruto Shippuden where Killer Bee is fighting Kisame.

Kuch Kuch Hota Hai is a Bollywood movie from 1998 that opens with a scene of cremation in an open field.

Pujas are a religious prayer ceremony in Hinduism held for any number of reasons.

Referenced in "Heart Rot": in trees, heart rot is a fungal disease that causes the decay of wood at the center of the trunk and branches. Fungi enter the tree through wounds in the bark and decay the heartwood. The diseased heartwood softens, making trees structurally weaker and prone to breakage.

The section three epigraph comes from Kaveh Akbar's poem "Pilgrim Bell."

The *gayatri* mantra is a prayer in Hinduism.

Durga and Shiva, mentioned in "Divine Contrapuntal" are both Hindu deities.

"From Under the Cork Tree" is a Fall Out Boy album title.

Pandit is a Hindu priest.

Previsouly Published Poems

Thank you to all the journals and literary magazines where the following poems appeared for the first time sometimes in different versions.

incantation to the departed, Barrelhouse, 2019

astral ashes, Glass: A Journal of Poetry, 2020

You've Gone Pink, HAD, 2021

Unripe Child, The Hellebore, 2021

88-01 88th Street, Hayden's Ferry Review, 2021

From Under the Cork Tree, No Contact Mag, 2022

Jellyfish Girl, Honey Literary, 2022

In Sixth Grade a Boy Calls me Octopus Hair, Honey Literary, 2022

my heart is a slippery fish, Honey Literary, 2022

i am unfit to raise daughters, Mid-American Review, 2022

self-portrait as manic episode, Whale Road Review, 2023

On Good Tongues, Chicago Quarterly Review, 2023

Crimson Girl, Prairie Schooner, 2023

Reciprocity, Prairie Schooner, 2023

i am unfit to raise daughters, reprinted, Mag 20/20, 2023

Acknowledgements

This book would not exist without the unwavering belief of many.

To my thesis director, mentor, and friend, Melissa Crowe, for never kicking me out of your office and seeing something in my work I couldn't see in myself, I am grateful every day to have met you. To Sayatani Dasgupta for reminding me that brown women are slated to take over the world, thank you for including me in your world domination plans, you are someone I aspire to be one day. To Anna Lena Bell Philips for showing me what softness in poetry can look like, your gentleness lent itself to many of these poems and my first graduate workshop with you welcomed me into a space that nurtured me from the get go and I'll always be thankful for you.

To the University of North Carolina MFA program, this book was built from the ground up in your care. Every class, every person I brushed elbows with, every person that ever listened to me read a poem aloud, you all helped give this book wings. Thank you to the following people for varying levels of poetic care, coffee, a laugh, or some shared moment over those three years: Andy Meyer, Ryleigh Wann, Hannah Bridges Horn, Lauren Fulcher, Noelle Powers, Stephanie Beckner, Michael Colbert, Jon Elofson, Emily Lowe, J.T. Smith, Ryan Varadi, Courtney Justus, Christopher Sturdy, Amanda Ake, Laura Traister, Victoria Hill, EJ Schwartz, Alston Tyer, Abby Logue, Nathan Conroy, Jamie Tews, Lashaun Noel, Cassie Mannes Murray, and Miriam Cone.

A more direct thank you to Tyler Anne Whichard and Katherine O'Hara for not only entering my life during that program, but for every afternoon you spent eating dinner on my floor. Every fire pit and game night. For every Facetime call and trip since. You both are my forever people and I thank the universe every day for bringing you to me.

To Susquehanna University for being the place that started my drive toward thinking this writing life was actually something I could want, could chase, could have. Monica Prince, Glen Retief, Karla Kelsey, Catherine Dent-Zobal thank you for your instruction and belief. To Madison Clark, for your unbelievable support of me after all these years. Dallas Aden, for being my absolute number one fan. Hope Martin, for your friendship and ranting and reminiscing. Those four years were my place of becoming.

To the Tin House Summer Workshop and Nate Marshall, thank you for seeing worth in these poems before I could and pushing me to see beyond myself.

To the Stadler Center for Poetry and Literary Arts for seeing me as capable and brimming. Your fellowship gave me the space to grow and submit this book and really see all I could be. And now I'm back in your grasp and even still you are gifting me more than I could ever verbalize. Chet'la Sebree, Joe Scapellato, Andy Ciotola, K.A. Hayes, thank you.

To the amazing writers that took the time to write blurbs for this collection I hold so close to my heart, Melissa Crowe, Rajiv Mohabir, Meg Day, Eduardo C. Corral. Thank you for your care with these words. For gifting me your words.

To Tyler Pufpaff and the whole Variant Literature team. Thank you for choosing this book amongst so many others. Thank you for seeing the worth in these words. For putting the time and effort into bringing this body of work into the world. I'm so grateful to have you as the press for my debut collection.

To my Discord girls, who are so much more than Discord girls these days. We found each other against all odds, on the internet, through anime. It wasn't until I had your love did I realize it was what I'd been looking for my entire life. I am who I am because of you. You've supported me unconditionally, been there through all the lowest points, and cheered me on in ways beyond belief. Carrington Wigfall, Qamar Samatar, Candace Seda, Lauren Keith, Mallory McRae, Gracious Villalobos, Jax Lilly, Nina Dudko, Addy Taylor, Lynndy Le, Gabrielle Morales, Rachel Silva, Ranjeeka Sharma, Julianne Lin, Abby Abebefe, Gabby Niko, Julia Ladson, Jalea Finklestein, Cat Gao, Kayla Hansen, Leah Nicole, Heather Johnson, Bri Hackett, Kristina Kekc, Mel Ngo, Tori, Yue, Lina Rone, J'Lee Christy, Rebecca Rhodes, Meg Johnson, Stacey Morales. Thank you for loving me and for letting me love you. I wouldn't have been able to love myself enough to finish this book if it hadn't been for you.

Katherine Luetters, Davis Holladay, Rachel Fisher, Cara Dowzicky, Heather Mena-Carias, Ricky Rodriguez, Sarah Ghazal Ali, Susan Nguyen, Sofia Aguilar, Kayla Peebles, luna rey hall, Sam Herschel Wein–thank you for your friendship in all their varying forms, it sustains me.

To my family. To my grandmother for being my first religion, this book wouldn't be what it is without you. To my brothers, for letting me be their older sister, you were the first things in this life I learned to care for. To my father, for teaching me how to care.

And lastly, to my mother, for everything. Without you I wouldn't be a poet. I wouldn't be a person. This book is possible because of everything you gave me, taught me. You gave me the love of the written word and really, what chance did I have? You made me a poet. Everything I am comes from you. There will never be enough language in this world to tell you how much I love you. Thank you. Thank you. Thank you.

About the Author

Jessica Nirvana Ram is an Indo-Guyanese first generation daughter of immigrants. She earned her MFA from the University of North Carolina Wilmington and her BA from Susquehanna University. Jessica was the 2022-23 Stadler Fellow in Literary Arts Administration. Her chapbook *rebuilding the temple* was published with Interrobang Press in 2018. Her work appears in Prairie Schooner, Hayden's Ferry Review, and Passages North. She is currently the Director of Sticky Fingers at Honey Literary, and also a poetry reader for Okay Donkey Magazine and Split Lip Magazine. Her chapbook *in the aftermath* was published with Prismatica Press in 2024. Jessica works as the Publicity and Outreach Manager for the Stadler Center for Poetry and Literary Arts at Bucknell University and presently lives in Lewisburg, PA.

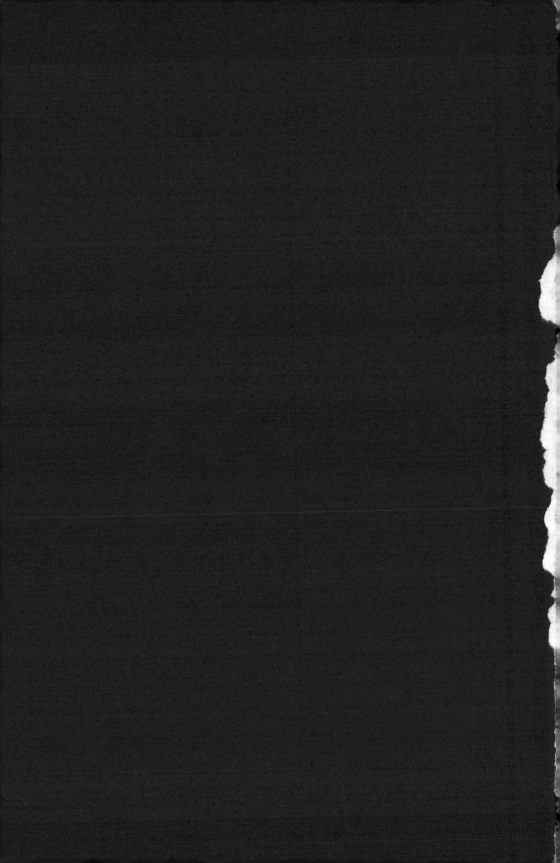